MW01452636

I Can Make Walls Talk

Poetry & Spoken Word

Foreword By Gail Morrison

Hewell Publishing

I Can Make Walls Talk © Utronda "AUDACIOUS" Wilson 2009

Audaciously Speaking

All rights reserved. This book or parts thereof may not be reproduced or utilized in any form or by any means; electronic or mechanical, including photocopying, recording, or by any information storage system, without permission in writing from the Author.

Selected Poems and Spoken Word by Utronda "AUDACIOUS" Wilson

ISBN 978-156870633-7

Cover Designer: Chad @ Wicks Designs (Dallas, Texas)
www.wicksdesigns.com

Editor: Katrina Dewalt (Arlington, Texas)

Cover Photo By: Cher Musico (Lewisville, Texas)
www.musicoroots.com

Wall Photos By: Audacious

Contacting Audacious:

audaciouslyspeaking@yahoo.com

www.myspace.com/icanmakewallstalk

HEWELL PUBLISHING

DEDICATION

written in memory of my father.....

My Father's Philosophy:

*"A man can work hard all his life and gain nothing;
but he can apply a single moment to his dream and accomplish the world"*.

Rest in Peace

Mr. E. V. "Jug" Wilson Jr.
November 9, 1946 – March 3, 2009

Foreword

As a speaker, when I sit under the voice of this powerful and profound young woman, I anticipate my spirit to be lifted, challenged and enlightened. I am never disappointed! In her giftedness, she connects deeply with her audience often matriculating in the hidden recesses of their souls. She has done it again! This time with her written words. The words of her soul which infuse life. The words of her heart which polarize often-harsh realities. The words of her spirit paint pictures for the mind, like the artist's brush does for the canvas. Words that are so colorful and vivid they can not be ignored. Words you can not help but see, hear and feel. Words which massage the mind spiritually, emotionally, psychologically and intellectually. Words so alive and invigorating, with such dynamic vibrations, it feels as if even the walls are talking!

Written By: *Gail Morrison*
Co-Founder Graceway Church, Speaker & Entrepreneur

i - The Foundation:
the basis on which something is grounded

Photo By: Audacious

Untitled # 1

I was born into a wayward world, an enslavement world
a hateful, conniving, bush filled manipulative world.

A GOD CREATED WORLD!

Marcus Garvey, Rosa Park, I have a dream, desegregation
slave dungeon, black on black crime, white on black crime,
because you're black and I hate you world
sit on the back of the bus world.

Prisons filled with black fathers, brothers and sons world
a devious world, let's go back to Africa world

ten kids in a three bedroom house eating out the same bowl world
hide and go seek playing and double Dutch, hopscotch, get in house
before the street lights come on world.

Preachers teaching but not believing world
folks in church stomping and jumping around but not HOLY filled world.

I cant get a job because my name LaShunda, Dre, Alexus, Felica, or
Tomeka
so I go by my middle name world
Mississippi raised and I want to leave this cotton-picking to make money
world
making babies but not taking care of them but she mine world

Jealous, two faced, back stabbing,
I want those rims but don't have a job NOR car world
always wanting what the next man has, nothing better world!

Nikki, Claude, Langston, Sojourner, Booker T, Venus, Serena, MJ, Madam CJ, Martin, Malcolm all stood up world and one day my little niece JORDYN MARIE will one day stand up world.
Tupac was a voice for the Negro teen so let us kill him world
KKK in the black Deep South world
an Isis Paper world.

You walk like this and I walk like that
locks, twists, relaxers and braids to the back
Brooks Brothers suit wearing, noose tie tying, Stacy Adams, Kenneth Cole, Ralph Lauren, Louis Vuitton, Gucci, Burberry and Hilfiger wearing
but who are these cats I am wearing
My people designing but I am not wearing world.

She thinks she got it going on world but the *truth* about the matter is that she's a ten and you all are just some haters world.

Mis-Education of the Negro world
Queen Nzinga world
Reality TV piloting black folks like we are foolish, stupid, and or ignorant world

I want to cut of social security but the U S of A is under attack I need to be fixing this world.

Kitchen curling, hot combing, flips, dips, CD and DVD burning
this is my hustle make money world; going to class high and haven't learn a thing world,
in college because it was the right thing to do world
don't know my history, where I am from, who I am, so I don't know where I am going world

But the truth about the matter is that *I was sitting at work when I wrote this world*!

The Revolution (Haiku)

the revolution
will be televised when we
open our eyes wide

The Exchange with Destiny

I have a few minutes to stand behind this mic:

So tonight, I just might tell you about the time
I exchanged words, with destiny.

There were no strings attached, no obligations, only mental relations.

She was as beautiful as the orange moon off 45 South,
She had teeth that sparkled truth from her mouth,
She was my first and I knew that she would definitely be my last,
Because she was the one who put letters on the heart on my cast.

She was destined, to be destiny.

Now, I didn't understand the fine print at the bottom of the page,
But lying down with her allowed me to release my rage.
Because she, had patience and I, was the patient,
And at that time only paper, pencil leads and black ink was my medication;
As destiny was the writer of this little lost girl's life prescription.

At 12 years old, embellishing hell to make her fell better,
and I was okay with that.
But she wanted me to be honest with myself because she knew the cards I was dealt.

So she decided to sit and cry along my bedside waiting for me to realize my true destiny with paper, pencil leads and black ink.

At 14 years old she wrote short stories about her life;
each one different from the next,

But similar because she dreamed of magical places with butterflies and fishing nets.

Now I know you may be confused and wonder how the two compare, but trust me,
Destiny gets it, while sitting eating strawberries from trees that birth pears.

But she continued to cry along my bedside waiting for me to realize my true destiny with paper, pencil leads and black ink.

QUEEN

Quintessentially unique, extravagantly exquisite and she has never given up on her dreams; because she is Q.U.E.E.N.

She will always be Mama's Angel and Daddy's Little Girl; but today, she wants take on the world and she can

She has the power to move freely throughout this chessboard of life, because she holds rank.

She has never needed beauty pageants to define her status because throughout the hardships she surpassed the ill masses.

She is Dallas's Elite and can't be defeated.

She's the female chieftain, the goddess with power of a Viking - hailing from the south coast and knowing more than most.

In a card game she flushes out imitators and perpetrators

Her philosophy in life is "*If you are who you say you are - A SUPERSTAR- have no fears only passions to drive yourself have past insanity to success, never needing help not rest - only intent to get rich,*"

NOT money though because that can be spent and nothing is more valuable than knowledge heaven sent.

She is the answer to your questions,
She is the right to your wrong,
she has fight in her,
she is the beginning to your end,
she is the holy oil for your sins,

she is your lover and your friend.

She is Quintessentially Unique, Extravagantly Exquisite and she has
Never given up on her dreams:

Because She Is Q.U.E.E.N.

Written for Every Strong Woman

Lack of Self Consciousness

Willie lynching in Mississippi on Timberland trees still exist in this century,

Feet dangling over moist red soil of the Delta.

Don't you hear that gasping for air

And you best not dare touch that noose because if you do then he'll shoot;

Because you decided to move in a direction that was not approved for you

And Thomas Jefferson said it best when they left us invisible

Invisible to freedom and you're dumb if you think differently because

This life isn't for free; its for rent.

So be careful of what you are spending.

So take off that Gucci, better yet spell Gucci,

Now do not get me wrong I am all about you bettering yourself

But let's get real,

When you finish dishing out your welfare check

How much of your self-worth will you have left?

We may as well send ourselves to hell because we are beginning to smell ourselves

And what do you expect a country to do for you that you can do for self

So do not get mad at me when the noose gets tighter

Because I'm just writer of this lack of self consciousness

And you are the inviter of this lack of self consciousness

And I know you wish that I would just quit telling you the truth but that is something that I just can't do!

So I Dream

I never believed in fairytales

So I dream

I dream outside the box,
I dream that I have the key to unlock the mind of every 5 year old
Sitting in kindergarten classes with crayon in hand
Scribbling outside the box
Because fairytales have endings so eventually, they stop

So I dream

I dream unto to blank pages
Filling composition notebooks
With metaphoric aspirations
Because this pen is my salvation
And this ink is my motivation
And fairytales are simply
Fictitious explanations,

So I dream

I dream so vividly
That one day Ray Charles, Stevie Wonder and my sister
Can see through my eyes
Because the soul of man never dies
It only cries out with passion
And fairytales are so unreal I wonder, where's the real passion

So I dream

I dream for eight year olds and their thoughts
That have been misplaced and laced
With false representations of a future
Holding them back not to be leaders but to be losers

So I dream

I dream that I rearranged the constellation and renamed each star
Jackson, Jordyn, Aniya, Mallory, Randle, Chloe, Reagan, Tally, Talon,
and the list can go on

Because dreams grow strong
And I'm not a mother,

But these are my seeds and I need them to breathe

So I dream,

So that they can believe!

The Evolution of Spoken Word

Sometimes we get so consumed with everything around us that we forget what is important: consumed with filth and lies that we do not realize our individual potentiality.

Jonzing for the Jones but we should be *jonzing* for clarity.

Clarity of a clear state of mind allowing time to take it course but of course, we fail tap into our intellect to set ourselves free.

Letting wings spread and minds embrace what has been laid out in front of us and no one said the road wouldn't be rough because if it wasn't then there wouldn't be an us; so when will get enough to just stand up for something that makes a little sense to you.

Sometimes we get so consumed with everything around us that we forget what is important: consumed with filth and lies that we do not realized that life is taking us over.

And we are not getting any younger only older, so why not wiser; so please allow me sometime to penetrate your mind with some uplift - none of that filth.

You all I'm Audacious and I was God fearing built – and all the prophets had in on *this creation*, They just put me here to do some mind stimulating and I'm tired of waiting.

I'm just dribbling poems trying to shake pass Satan, dunking on haters and they are not understanding because they are simply motivating courage to dwell up in these bones and I wont stop until I reach the throne to exchange verses about this mind pollution because I'm just trying to start a spoken word evolution.

And yes, it may be futuristic but if I don't utilize my gifts then consider me ridiculous.

So understand this, it is the E. V. O. L. U. T. I. O. N. and if not now, WHEN?

ii - The Bricks:
hard block used for construction

Photo By: Audacious

I M STANDING

Tonight, I'm standing for more than white t shirts and sagging pants,
I'm standing
I'm standing for more than grilled out mouths of cavities and filth,
I'm standing
I'm standing for more than jig a boo dances to beats with words that don't make sense but only disgrace and enslave, I'm standing
I'm standing for more those than those that rock dread lock but their minds are locked on the wrong things,

I'm Standing!

I'm standing for more,
I'm standing for future generations of little brown boys and little brown girls, khaki boys and khaki girls, Haitians and even Ghanaians,
I'm standing
I'm standing for my beliefs so that one day this land will finally be considered our land,

I'm standing for proper education for all,
I'm standing for cancer research for all,

I'm standing because I was told that if I don't stand for something then I stand for nothing at all,

I'm Standing!

I'm standing for equal equality for blacks, white, lesbians, gays, atheist and even slaves
I'm standing so that the chains of slavery will be cut free
I'm standing so that you will judge me for me, I'm standing
I'm standing for the four little girls in the Alabama bombing
I'm standing for my people in Mississippi slumming
I'm standing for Barrack Obama even for Hillary Clinton,
I'm standing because my people are still dealing mentally with Willie Lynching,

I'm standing!

I'm standing for the thirty three souls in the Virginia Tech Massacre,
I'm standing because I know that there's a hidden AIDS cure, I'm standing!

I'm standing for the six little black boys in Jena, LA and if you don't believe that that's today's black reality then why am I standing but I'm standing because this is how I feel and if I don't stand, WHO WILL?

Fallen (Haiku)

I woke up today
and realized that I had
fallen beyond love

Suicide

He wrote his suicide note in crayon
Packed his soul inside his lunch box
Looked at himself in the mirror and said

"*I can't stop*"

Because life didn't exist to him anymore
And he was only two times four

And you, you were too busy
Instead of being a mother, you were being a whore

But I don't blame you I hold you accountable
Because you brought him into this world
And took him out
So actually, you are a cannibal

You may as well have trimmed his limbs and devoured him
When all he wanted was for you to empower him
But you were too blind to see this angel
Because if it wasn't laying on your back
That was not your angle

And you were suppose to be the one to protect him from danger
But when he came into your room that night
And told you that the monsters in his closet was making him anger
You treated him as if he was a stranger

But I don't blame you I hold you accountable
Because you brought him into this world
And took him out

So actually, you are a cannibal

You may as well have split open his chest and laid him to rest
Because you never gave him the chance to be his best

And you never tried to make your old man quite
Because all you were worried about was your next fix

But the reality of this conversation is thick
Usually I do not curse but right now, I am pissed
So I'm going to call you what you are and that's a b__

I just wish that I could watch you hang yourself

Because last night your baby boy took his last breathe
Besides the depression, the doctor said he was in prefect health

But all you were worried about was yourself.

Dare To Disturb (Haiku)

I dared to disturb
the universe, verse by verse
and found truth within.

Needs Verses Wants

I stood there in an open field of orchids and I breathed you
I inhaled your being
I tasted your soul
And was tempted to reach out and hold you.

Hold you like it was the last time.
Hold you like Jesus held Noah before the storm.
I need you.

I need you like rose petals needs water
Like clocks needs time
Like oceans needs waves
And like butterflies need wings
I stood there.

I stood there with joy in one hand and hope in the other;
As I knelt to plant a lifetime of love at your feet.
I blew kisses at the skyline and thanked heaven for sending you into my life.
My heart skipped a beat but your soul collided with mine and pumped life into my existence.
I stood there.

I stood there on day 3 of our conversation
As you told me that sometimes in life – the things that you want; you get
And the things that you need; you sometimes forget
So today I'm turning my needs into wants because I want you.

So if I have to stand in a field of orchids – I will stand there.

I will stand there in a field of orchids and I will breathe you
I will inhale your being
I will taste the nectar of your soul
And I will reach out and touch you
I will hold you like it was the first time
I will hold you like Jesus held Noah before the storm;
Because I don't need you...

I want you.

I thought about putting a poem on this page,
but sometimes my words are silent.

My Answer

She asked me if I was a racist.

So I stood there and looked her in her eyes.

I saw myself look inside myself and for a moment,
I felt a fit of rage.

Because why should I explain the me I am,
why should I explain the way I am,
the way I feel
or even the way I see this world in which we have succumb,
surrendered and gracefully submitted to.

Okay, so then I calmed myself down and decided to answer her
question that she obviously needed an explanation to.

My answer.

No, I am not a racist only a clear observer of what has been done to my
fore fathers, mothers, sisters, and brothers.

I do not hate nor dislike or have racist thoughts towards those who are
not of my own.

I UNDERSTAND what my past is, was and will always be.

I UNDERSTAND the way he, the man of not my own feels, thinks or
sees of ME, US and OURS.

Of mine, of the Black Afro-American, a history that is so long and painful
I READ to understand not to be a racist!

BUT then she asked me if I was a racist.

And for a moment I felt a fit of rage.

Why should I explain the me I am,
why should I explain the way I am,
the way I feel
or even the way I see this world in which we have succumb,
surrendered and gracefully submitted to.

So this is to her question that she needed an explanation to;
I answered.

No. I am not a racist, only do I understand that ONLY I CAN!

Why should I sit back and wait on someone else to give to my churches, my schools, my corner stores, my colleges, my businesses, my people and mine.

So do not take my RECIPROCITY as racism, take it as MY ANSWER!

My Heart is in Limbo

My heart is in limbo,
in this state trying to figure out whether to feel again.
Because the feelings that I have for you are so real,
but I feel tears every time I think of you.

And yes, we are still friends
but I don't know how friendly I will be with you
because I'm missing you, needing us,
but my heart is on the edge; one step from being dead.

My heart feels trapped in this oblivion state of confinement with no where to go...
this is nonsense and we both know it.
We are both in a position of pushing love away that we are destined to blow it.

Why?

So now, I am asking the questions:
What is love if you never love?

How will you ever know love if you continue to run from it?

Lastly, I' m feeling you and I take it you are feeling me,
so are you ready to allow yourself to be loved with no boundaries, no limits, no elements of surprise, just free...

It's Simple

I answered,
just love me for who I am
nothing more,
simply
for me.

I Can Take You Higher

I can take you higher

These were the only words that she heard before she placed that needle to her vein
Because all she was worried about was releasing her pain
and nothing else mattered; she was a battered woman of the night that lived her moments fighting for just another transaction on the pavement

I can take you higher

These words kept her moving to a new beat each day,
She knew of nothing else; this was the environment that invited her
And she graciously accepted without dialogue of what she would possibly compromise.

She gave into the addiction that caused her to flat line, BEEP...............

I can take you higher

Suddenly, her heart began to pump breathe into her existence.
After twenty minutes of coding her body resisted. She continued subconsciously to pull her body to its expiration.

She knew that if her soul was restored that she would have to make a commitment; to live her life to its full potential. Because he was explaining to her within her outer body experience that "*He Could Take Her Higher* (singing)"

This Girl

I met this girl last Saturday
We went to church on Sunday
Had sundaes on Monday
And sat in the park reading poetry on Tuesday
We had fellowship on Wednesday
Exchanged war stories on Thursday and
On Friday... well, you know...

We got past the informalities
All representatives were laid to the side
I decided I wanted to know this girl
Maybe even show this girl a different way
The further we went
The deeper she saw my soul and I found myself exposed without shield or sword to hide behind...

Something about her shook me,
But she never mistook me
Everywhere she was, I wanted to be
This girl was fine and I wanted to make her mine but I just couldn't get her to settle

She challenged me to be more
Always surrounding me with reflections of self
I began to see what was laid out for me
Experiencing life as it was meant to be

This girl was God sent and purposely designed
And as I said before I wanted to make her mine.

Yes, outwardly, you saw beautiful brown eyes and seductive lips but this was not what made me fall for her,
When I asked her what would make her mine,
She said your heart, your soul and your mind
Sometimes at night when she would rest
I would check to see if she wore an S on her chest

This girl was blazing, daring, original and amazing
Fearless, relentless, reckless and crazy
Bold bronzing and even bodacious,

Who was this girl?

You know her as Audacious.

Fall in love with yourself sometimes....

Our Final Goodbye (Haiku)

We said goodnight not
knowing that it would be the
last time we would speak

Rest in Peace Dad

"*with his death, I transformed*"

iii - The Transformation:

a complete change, usually into something with an improved appearance or usefulness

Photo By: Audacious

The Perfect Storm

The winds were powerful
spiraling around the center of low; in degree and intensity
Its elevation was small and yes, low in pitch and in frequency.

I was trapped in a large black funnel hanging down from a storm cloud; vision blurry, soul broken and heart in pieces after laying my existence out on the line of love's hemisphere.

Coming from the Latin word "*tonore*" meaning thunder
I'd wonder why me
Having to be whisked away in whipping winds back and forth,
because I have learned that this to you has been a game
So what does thunder with no lighting means? NOTHING
There is no difference because rotating and or twisting winds are the same

The force you used my elders would describe it as a train plunging from its tracks with death as the conductor; ready for destruction, with no direct sense of direction. Its only aim, do it with perfection!
Because you have done this before

Entering one world so peacefully

That night the clouds were clear
And I could see the constellation of Orin's Belt
We laid there in the lawn staring out at the abyss and then suddenly the earth was still and silent

Standing there alone I then felt the piercing winds and hailstorms combined with 300 mile per hour speeds headed right toward my heart
Then I remembered, I stated to my best friend just weeks ago
That I did not want feeling like this
Because I had broken so many hearts in the past that presently my past was catching up with me.

Now trapped in a black violent cloud unable to breathe and all I wanted was to be like Dorothy in the Wiz of Oz and breathe
But you held me there,
Consciously uprooted me from the earth's core and tortured me
Hurled my heart like overturning a diesel to its backside
Now my feeling are destroyed
And all I wanted to do was escape with what little pride I had left

But you insisted to form because you were at the peak of your season and geographically I was placed in your path to receive the result of your outbreaks
Now I'm confused; I remember having the conversation about being authentic,
Now knowing, that was fake
But with this one I didn't get the tornado sirens or warnings that a storm was near
My detection was off balanced
So now, my heart has been devastatingly damaged

You left me with my exterior walls blown away and piles of the debris of our existence, laying there. So speaking to universe "*where's the tips for this*" because I now need more than just a 1st aid kit, maybe some can food, a can opener, battery operated radio, flash light, bottled water, protective clothing and even written instructions because *if there is a next time*, I'll save my heart from your destruction.

Predictability (Haiku)

I'm so predictable
that I'm unpredictable
that's who I am.

My Poetry Has a Purpose

I have sailed the Atlantic Ocean starting at the coast of the Gambia

I walked the streets of Banjul while listening to beats of talking drums of

all shapes and sizes,

I slept in the village of Tafo

I exchanged graces with the Kings concubines after praying the mass of

Senegal.

I shopped along side African Queens deciphering between oil

paintings and craved statues with images of myself

I exhale....

And release life into the air

Armoring myself with knowledge, power and inner strength

Letting go past hurts, failures and lost

Simply gaining power through believing in me,

Having faith and a vision to see past others insecurities

to judge me,

because I know who my father is and he created me simply to win

I inhale....

While accepting his guidance to minister through spoken words,

empowering lives with haikus, conjunctions and broken verbs because

my poetry has a purpose...

Untitled # 2

Singing:

"*Have mercy on me Lord,*
I just cant seem to get it right
Please don't give up on me Lord,
Have favor in your sight.

I don't have to sin everyday
One day I'll be just like Christ,
But only if you have mercy on me"

Spoken Words:

It felt like I was standing on top of a cardboard box in the middle of the rain
Blaming myself for all the struggles that I had been through
And at that moment I didn't know what to do
So I picked up a pen and I started to write
Actually, I started to fight and take back what was rightfully mine.
He whispered in my ears and told me it was time to write words
That would keep a nation feed.
He opened up the Bible and so I read first Timothy chapter 4 in its entirety; and after reading those verses I was able to see a clearer vision of my path.
Because he told me that his teachings were mine to have
As he knelled down to my feet and told me that no one could ever defeat (me)
As he blew breathe into my bones
After handing me myrrh, franken scents and gold
He told me to take a stand because he already blessed me with a mic and a plan

Singing:

"Have mercy on me Lord,
I just cant seem to get it right
Please don't give up on me Lord,
Have favor in your sight.

I don't have to sin everyday
One day I'll be just like Christ,
But only if you have mercy on me"

Forgiveness

She was left out and dealt a messed up hand; yet if she had the chance to play her cards right
then I just might not be standing on this stage full of something to say
because when I think about it I know
that's why I write this way, that way and anyway my heart desires
because through her I spit fires
because she has some dungeons that need to be burned down

at nine years old, looking into her eyes
I saw a woman who wanted to drown but she didn't
she wanted more

so like wings of an eagle she decided to soar;
but with ten kids in a household and a marriage about to fold
I was told that mommy needs you and that mommy will not leave you

and I was barely turning ten and couldn't comprehend the message
behind the message and at the point the marriage was becoming messy

you see my sibling who is above me is actually my half
and mother, she decided to have her marriage just the way that it was
because in those days marriages weren't founded on love and you were lucky if found it and sometimes it got so crazy

I wondered,
why didn't she leave him
and why did she believe him
and why did she do everything in her power to please him

now I am turning twelve and going through hell
developing rage inside,

so I needed an outlet
so that's when I feel in love with stages
started going through phases
started stepping up to mics ripping page after page after page

and he wondered why I was behaving the way that I was
and everything he asked of me I did the opposite of
in spite of him because *I hated him for her*

but it wasn't until recently that I realized that she adored him
and that there was more to him

so as she laid there in the hospital bed
him kissing her forehead and gently whispering in her ear
baby I need you so please don't leave me

that's when I saw the six-year-old little boy who cried himself to sleep at night simply because he needed someone to hold him

and that's when I saw the eight-year-old little boy who went out into cotton fields to pick cotton because that was his place

and that's when I saw the ten year old little boy who couldn't read nor write but had so much fight in him,

so I realized that I could not continue to deny him,

so tonight on *this* stage
behind *this* mic
in front of *these* people

Daddy, I apologize!

SHERO (Haiku)

She walks with confidence
nothing can stop her
she is, SUPERWOMAN!

I Am Still Standing

I am standing because my foundation was laid at birth
Through screams of labor pains and hurt
My life, I live through a possible death,
Not realizing then that I was born into wealth
He took what was already inside of me to fix me
Because the blood transfusions didn't make me free
And yet, I was not broken, *I was broken*
Wrecked inside to be ill conditioned at five
Nevertheless, God's plan allowed me to survive

I'm still standing, because my words like bricks and made of Christ
So I can endure the force of any might, stronghold or even temptation

Because my father has my back and this pen is my salvation
And one day my words will reach thousands of generations,
While healing souls in a million nations,
I'm still standing

I am still standing while breathing life through ink stains
So that others may only interpret my spiritual wealth,
because if I do not live, then you may as well consider me death.

I'm still standing; after long teary nights on my bathroom floor
Praying to my father that I did not want to hurt any more
But he kept me there because secretly I wasn't ready to move
So he took away my option to choose
Because he presented me with chance after chance
And at that time in life I did dance after dance
Until that day I had made up my mind
That living in sin had taking up to much of my time

And if I had to say it in another language or sign
I shouted "*Lord forgive me just one more time*"

Because I have learned, that Favor is not fair
So, I dared to disturb the universe and found truth within
Got down on my knees and found truth within
Prayed and asked my father to forgive me of my sins
Deliver me from what impaired me within,
Lifted my hands to the heavens claiming victory and a win

And he did,

He took death and made life
Brought me from darkness to the light
Held me close and told me that everything would be alright
He showed me the truth and told me I could do anything I wanted to do
Even presented me with a HD (*High Definition*) preview,
All I had to do is live by faith and not by sight
Because I can do all things, through Christ,

Because I am Still Standing!

Afterthought:

It took a moment of devastation for me to find peace.

Morning after morning we wake up and start our daily routines in life. We conform to what we have been told is the way to get to the *American Dream*. However, I stand corrected. Now having found truth and courage inside myself, through believing and having faith, I know what blessed (*internally content; regardless of my external surroundings*) truly feels like.

Please remember, life's experiences will not be placed strategically in order. You will only find your rode map during the journey, whether good, bad and/or ugly.

About Audacious

Bold, daring, and courageous are all adjectives often used to describe Dallas' newest poet and author, Audacious. Birthed through the intoxicating waters of the Mississippi Delta, she has arrived to clearly and definitively make her mark on the literary world.

Growing up in Ruleville, Mississippi, the wild child of "Jug" and Christine Wilson, she discovered through life's hurdles that there is power in words. Audacious fell in love with the word early in life, first taking stage at the age of twelve while being inspired by her favorite author Nikki Giovanni. Life has lead her to travel around the world from Africa to New York spreading her positive messages of uplift and outreach.

In 2008, she catapulted her journey and founded Audaciously Speaking, dedicated to change and regeneration through spoken word. Often described as infectious, Audacious provides experiences through her revolutionary style of poetry. She has allowed her words to possess her taking stage at venues such as The Black Academy of Arts and Letters, The University of Texas at Arlington, Café Madrid, Embargo and Absinthe Lounge to name just a few. Her own Evolution of Spoken Word is an Annual Red Carpet event to raise literary awareness.

This year, Audacious does it all, launching the Back Pack Foundation to support schools with the supplies they need to equip today's youth to become tomorrow's leaders. She continues to be a motivational force both in the community and on stage. You have just experienced the one, the only, Audacious.

Thank You

To my **SPIRTIUAL FATHER**, thank you for covering me with your grace and mercy. Days that I wanted to give up, you showed up and showered me heavily with your presence. You surrounded me with family, friends, associates and even strangers who cared enough to motivate me when I built walls to hide behind. Words cannot express the joy and peace I have found in you. To my **FATHER**, rest in peace; thank you for being a MAN, a FATHER and a FRIEND. I know, *"the show must go on!"* To my **MOTHER**, thank you for being a woman that every woman wants to be! Your strength cannot be matched! To my **SIBLINGS** (Monique, Mellernea, Stephanie, Carolyn, Shantella, Thyeshia, Fugi, Eric and Telly), being the youngest of ten t aught me to be AUDACIOUS (lol). Thank YOU! What more can a girl ask for, you all are the best big sisters and brothers anyone can have. You all have played significant roles in my life that only you and I know of, so let us keep it that way (smile). Thank you for being the BEST. I Love You All. To **JORDYN MARIE,** thank you for showing how to love unconditionally. To all those in my corner that assisted with making this possible, **BIG THANKS** to: Nikki, Rasha, Altrese, Shawn, Shelly, Nakia, Varonda, Sharonda, Royalty, CHAD (Wicks Designs), Chyrstal (Hewell Publishing), Prudence The Isis, Calvin, AJ Houston, Romaro, Kia D (KEBNRadio.com), Venus, Wesley, Unique (*"It's A Movement"*) and Gail Morrison. To **EVERY** host, mc, dj, club owner, poet, singer, band member.....simply ALL ARTISTS... who allowed me to share a stage, club, lounge or just space with you...THANKS! You guys rock! To all those who have played a **VIP ROLE** in my life and have not been mentioned (you know who you are) THANKS A MILLION! Finally yet importantly, to my **YOUTH, SUPPORTERS**, **FANS**, **FAMILY** and **FRIENDS** without your open ears and hearts I could not go forward, THANK YOU!

Reviews

"What a matchless source! Speaking in volumes, she leaves the crowd wanting more, but not before they are filled with an amazing desire to enlighten themselves and others."

Monique Wilson
Sister & Stylist (Hair Elegance)
moni_wil09@yahoo.com

"Audacious is one of the boldest poets I have come to know. She is not the poet to come into a setting and conform to the every day song and dance."

Prudence the Isis
Actress & Spoken Word Artist
www.myspace.com/Prudencetheisis

*"Audacious is the only poet I know who can take the harsh realities of the world and wrap them in such a beautiful truth, like a rose...
All I can say is; I'll take a dozen."*

Calvin Sharp
Poet & Spoken Word Artist
carmel_intelligence@yahoo.com

Audaciously Speaking